Food I Love To Eat Too

For My Husband, ♥♥
Taster Extraordinaire & My Very Own Personal
Belief System. Love you My Darling!! xxx
For my Boys, Joe & Oscar, My Driving Force
& not to forget Harry the Dog & Sid the Cat.

For My Mum & My Nana, My Inspirers,
You are the ones who got me started. xx

For Tashy the best cake maker, wonderful &
amazingly brave friend I have ever known! xx

For Kate S, who we sadly lost to Breast Cancer,
think of you often Darling, Miss your beautiful face
& laugh x

For Helen SL, Karen M, Susie B, Karen WB & Kate L
for being my biggest champions & supporters!
Love you Ladies xx

For Ashleigh, for being my help, my rant buddy,
looking after me before & after the surgery, for being
such a Special Friend & so very bossy!!

And for My Dad, for just being My Dad! xx

Food I  To Eat Too

Lisa Liffen

I thoroughly enjoyed writing the first book, Food I Love To Eat, & I wanted to continue in the same vein so as long as I keep cooking, I will keep writing after all I am doing two of the things that I love doing the most! I still LOVE to cook, LOVE to eat & LOVE to FEED! I am so passionate about food & what my family eats. It is important that we all, especially children, get the best food available to us, & that good food doesn't have a big price tag attached to it. We have a 3 year old who eats Olives like Apples & Tomatoes like Strawberries. We have started his own little garden at home, so that he understands where his vegetables come from & how rewarding it can be growing & eating your own food. Children need to be involved in the kitchen as much as possible, so they learn how to cook great food rather than settling for processed rubbish that is all too easily available.

The concept of this book is exactly the same as the first book, get the recipe here & go on line to look for pictures, not just mine but other peoples. I am blogging most days now, **www.foodilovetoeat.com** so there should be something new on the website every day. I hope you enjoy cooking, not just for others, but for yourself & your family. Have fun being in the kitchen & looking the faces of the people you cook for!!!

Salads

Goats Cheese with Apple & Walnut Salad

SERVES 4

This is a simple salad, but so so yummy.

Ingredients

300g of Rocket Leaves, 200g of Whole Walnuts, 150g of Goats Cheese, 4 Pink Lady Apples, EVO, Lemon Juice & fresh Ground Black Pepper.

Method

Cut the Walnuts into quarters. Remove the Apple cores & thinly slice from top to bottom, leaving the skin on. Scatter the Rocket Leaves on a serving dish, repeat with the Walnuts & then the sliced Apple. Gently break up the Goats Cheese with your fingers, placing small pieces all over the Apple. Dress with a drizzle of EVO & Lemon Juice. Season with a touch of Ground Black Pepper.

Green Bean & Fennel Salad

SERVES 4

I love this made with Thin Green Beans, but you can use Broad Beans if you have them, especially of you have been lucky enough to have grown your own, something we will be attempting next year.

Ingredients

250g of Thin Green Beans, 2 Garlic Cloves, 1 Fennel Stalk, WWV, 10-20 Black Olives, EVO, Salt & Pepper.

Method

Boil the Kettle. Cut the tops & bottoms from the Beans. Place in a pan, add a tbsp. of salt & cover with boiling water. Return to the boil, reduce to a simmer until the Beans are tender but still have crunch. Place in a bowl of Iced Water for 5 minutes then drain. Slice on the angle into approx. 3 pieces per Bean. Place in a serving dish. Finely chop the Garlic, & place in a small bowl, add a pinch of Salt, 1tbsp. of WWV & 1 tbsp. of EVO. Pour over the Beans. Chop the Fennel as finely as you can & add to the dish, along with the Olives. Mix well & serve immediately. Great as a side for Chicken or Lamb.

Tomato Salad

SERVES 6-8

This makes a lot of Salad so it is brilliant for a Family BBQ or when you are having lots of people round. It's very fresh &

I'm sure you could blend it down & add a slug of Vodka. And of course it's great to mop up all the juices with bread!

Ingredients

1Kg of different sized & different coloured Tomatoes, 1 Large Red Onion, 1 Large White Onion, 2 Cucumbers, 4tbsp. of EVO, 4 tbsp. of Lemon Juice, 25 Large Mint Leaves, Salt & Pepper.

Method

Slice all the Tomatoes in half. Remove the seeds & cut the flesh into same size cubes. Place in a mixing bowl. Peel the Cucumbers, cut in half lengthways & scoop out the seeds. Cut into cubes & place in the mixing bowl. Peel the Onions, finely dice, adding to the Tomatoes & Cucumber. Finely slice the Mint Leaves & add to the mixing bowl. Cover with cling film & place in the Fridge for 1 hour or longer. Pour any watery juice away, Season with Salt & Pepper. Drizzle with EVO & Lemon Juice over the mix, get your hands in & gently toss. Transfer into a serving dish.

Feta Salad

SERVES 6

I have been to several of the Greek Islands & I always, enjoy a traditional Feta Salad. This is my take on it.

Ingredients

3 Large Tomatoes, 2 Cucumbers, 1 Small Red Onion, 150g of Feta Cheese, 4 tbsp. of OO, 1 tsp. Dried Oregano, 20 Black Olives, Salt & Pepper.

Method

Chop the Tomatoes & Cucumber in to cubes & place in a mixing bowl. Peel the Onion, cut in half & thinly slice, making into half-moons. Add to the bowl & mix well. Season with Salt to taste, cover with cling film & leave in the fridge until 10 minutes before serving. Mix again, drizzle with OO & thinly slice the Pepper lengthways & add. Shake half of the Oregano in to the bowl, mix again, & crumble the feta over the top, add the Olives & the remaining Oregano over the top. Serve immediately.

Melon, Mozzarella & Parma Ham Salad

SERVES 4

We had Mum & Dad over for dinner when I threw this together. We were laughing at Dad, who couldn't wait for me to take a photo, & just dove right in!! He knows what he likes.

Ingredients

1 Medium Cantaloupe Melon, 12 pieces of Prosciutto, 2 Large Mozzarella Balls, Wholegrain Mustard, Honey, EVO, Lemon Juice, Salt & Pepper.

Method

Slice the Cantaloupe in half & remove all the seeds. Cut each half into three pieces. Remove the skin by lying each piece on a countertop, & using a paring knife or similar follow the line of the skin of the Melon. Once all the pieces have had the skin removed, cut in to chunks. Place on a serving plate. Pull the Mozzarella apart into various size pieces & place on the plate with the Melon. Weave the Prosciutto around the pieces of Melon & Mozzarella. Put 2 tsp. of Wholegrain Mustard in a small bowl, add 2 tsp. of runny Honey, 1 tbsp. of EVO & 1 tbsp. of Lemon Juice. Mix together well. Taste, add a pinch of Salt & Pepper. If too sweet & more EVO & Lemon Juice, if too bitter add a little more EVO & Honey. Drizzle over the plate or you can simply leave on the side for everyone to help themselves. Serve with Mediterranean Bread.

Tabbouleh

SERVES 6

Tabbouleh can be made in so many different ways, this is my favourite but you can add as many different salad vegetables as you want & even Chicken or Prawns!

Ingredients

200g Fine Bulgar Wheat, 500ml of Hot Chicken Stock, 4 Tomatoes, 2 Cucumbers, 4 Spring Onions, 3 Garlic Cloves, Fresh Parsley, Fresh Mint, 2 Lemons, EVO, Salt & Pepper.

Method

Place the Bulgar Wheat in a bowl & pour over the Hot Chicken Stock. Cover with cling film & leave until all the liquid has been absorbed. Once the liquid has been absorbed pour into a sieve & gently press the Bulgar Wheat to squeeze out any excess. Cut each Tomato in half & remove the seeds. Repeat with the Cucumber. Place each Tomato half face down, cut in to cubes. Place the Cucumber face down, slice in half through the long middle & cut into cubes. Chop the Spring Onions, & finely chop the Garlic, a handful of chopped Parsley & shredded Mint Leaves. Mix all the ingredients in a large bowl, drizzle with EVO & the Juice of 2 Lemons. Mix well & add a little more EVO if too dry, but do not make too wet. Place in the fridge for an hour or two to chill, stir well before serving.

Avocado, Spinach & Pancetta Salad

SERVES 4

Ingredients

1 Large ripe Avocado, 125g of Chopped Pancetta, 1 bag of Baby Spinach, 1 tbsp. of Whole Grain Mustard, juice of ½ a Lemon, EVO, OO, Salt & Pepper.

Method

In a small bowl mix together the Mustard, the Lemon Juice & 6tbsp. of OO. Mix well & set aside. Add a small glug of OO to a frying pan & add the Pancetta, cook until golden. Pour onto kitchen roll to drain & allow to cool. Wash the Baby Spinach, dry & add to a serving dish. Scatter the Pancetta over the top of the Spinach. Peel the Avocado & cut into cubes, add to the serving dish & spoon the dressing over the top. Mix well & serve.

Tuna & Green Bean Salad

SERVES 4

Ingredients

OO, 2 Fresh Tuna Steaks, 2 Tomatoes, 1 Little Gem Lettuce, ½ Cucumber, 1 Garlic Clove, 2 Spring Onions, 100g of Long Green Beans, 75g of Black Olives, 3 Eggs, 2 tbsp. of Fresh Parsley, Salt & Pepper.

Method

Boil the kettle. Pour the boiled water into a pan & return to the boil. Add a large pinch of Salt. Add the Eggs, reduce to a simmer & cook for 8 minutes. Remove from the pan & place into iced water until you can hold them to peel. Whilst the Eggs are cooking, cut the Tomatoes into wedges, sprinkle with Salt & set aside. Slice the Cucumber & the Spring Onions & place in a serving bowl with the Green Beans, Olives, & Lettuce. Peel & cut the Eggs into wedges. Smash the Garlic Cloves & finely chop. Add a glug of OO to a small pan & cook the Garlic until soft, remove & allow to cool. Roughly chop the Parsley, mix with OO, Garlic & season. Add the Tomatoes to the bowl & mix well. Add the Parsley & Garlic. Coat the Tuna Steaks with OO, season with Salt & Pepper & cook on a griddle pan for 2-3 minutes each side. Allow to rest for 5 minutes & slice into a strips. Add the Eggs to the bowl & the Tuna strips & mix well. Season with Salt & Pepper & a little drizzle of OO.

Watermelon, Feta & Olive Salad

SERVES 4-6

This Salad is just so cool & the colours are beautiful.

Ingredients

EVO, ½ a Large Watermelon, 300g of Feta Cheese, 30 Black Olives & 30 Green Olives & Fresh Oregano Leaves (or 1 tbsp. of Dried Oregano)

Method

Cut the Watermelon into bite sized pieces removing all the Seeds. Place in a serving dish. Remove the Feta Cheese from the packets & place between 2 dry tea towels & pat dry. Crumble the Feta over the Melon, & sprinkle with Oregano. Drizzle with EVO & add the Olives.

Roasted Red Pepper Salad.

SERVES 6

This is lip smacklingly delicious.

Ingredients

EVO, 2 Red Peppers, 2 Yellow Peppers, 30g Capers, 20 Black Olives, 2 Garlic Cloves, 2 tbsp. Lemon Juice, Small Handful of Fresh Marjoram, a Pinch of Sugar, Salt & Pepper.

Method

Heat the grill to the high, lie the Peppers on a wire rack & place under the grill turning frequently until the skins are blackened & blistered. Remove from the wire rack & place in a sealable bag. Leave for 20 minutes until cool Take a Pepper from the bag, hold over a bowl, make a small incision in the base & gently squeeze out the juices. Peel off the skins & discard. Cut the Peppers in thin strips, arrange in a serving dish, add the EVO, Lemon Juice, chop the Garlic Cloves & add with the Sugar, Pepper Juices & a pinch of Salt to a bowl & mix well. Drizzle over the Peppers, scatter Capers, Olives & Marjoram. Best Served with Olive Bread.

Feta, Mint, Bean, Pistachio & Strawberry Salad
SERVES 6
Oh Wow!!! This is amazeballs! Just place it in the middle of your table as a starter & watch what happens!

Ingredients
500g of Fine Green Beans, 500g of Feta Cheese, 500g of Strawberries, 5 tbsp. of Pistachio Nuts, 1 Large Handful of Fresh Mint Leaves, 2 tbsp. of OO, 1 tbsp. of Dijon Mustard, 2 tbsp. OO, Salt & Pepper.

Method
Mix the Vinegar, Sugar, Mustard & Salt in a bowl, slowly add the OO until it comes together, cover & place in the fridge. Boil a pan of salted water, add the Green Beans for 2 minutes, drain & place into a bowl of iced water. Remove the top part of the Strawberries & cut in half. Add to a bowl along with the Pistachios, shred the Mint Leaves & add. Drain the Beans, add to the Strawberries & Nuts & mix well. Add a little of the dressing to the Beans, just enough to evenly coat them & mix well. Transfer into a serving dish & break the Feta all over the top of the dish & season with freshly ground Black Pepper.

Chickpea Salad

SERVES 6

Ingredients

2 tins of Chickpeas, 1 Red Onion, 4tbsp. Fresh Parsley, Juice of 1 Lemon & 6tbsp. EV, Salt & Pepper.

Method

Finely chop the Parsley. Add the Parsley, EVO & Juice of a Lemon to a bowl. Season with Salt & Pepper & mix well. Peel the Onion, cut in half, slice & flake. Add to the bowl. Drain the Chickpeas & wash. Add to the bowl & mix together.

Prawn & Couscous Salad

SERVES 4

This is best with the fattest juiciest Prawns you can find.

Ingredients

500g of Cooked Tiger Prawns, 100g of Couscous, 500ml of Hot Chicken Stock, 400g of Cherry Tomatoes, 1 Garlic Clove, 1 Large Red Pepper, Fresh Parsley, Juice of 1 Lemon, ½ tsp. of Dried Oregano, OO, Salt & Pepper.

Method

Pour the Couscous into a bowl, cover with Chicken Stock & cover with cling film. Leave for about 15minutes until the stock has been absorbed. Finely chop the Garlic, cut the Tomatoes in half & the Red Pepper into chunks. Add a glug of OO to a large frying pan, & add the Garlic, Tomatoes & Red Pepper to the pan, until softened then add the Prawns & stir well. Season with Salt, Pepper & Oregano. Once cooked remove from the heat. Finely chop the Parsley. Add the Couscous & Vegetables to a bowl. Mix well. Sprinkle with 4tbsp. of Chopped Parsley & the juice of the Lemon. Mix well again & serve.

Soups

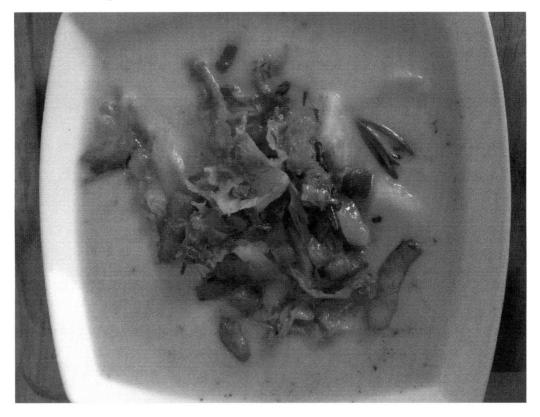

I love soup. Everyone has a favourite soup. I have about 12! I was raised on soup. My favourite as a child was Tomato Soup & my Sister's was Oxtail, which I find amusing now as she has been a vegetarian for over 20 years!! Soup was for lunch on Saturday whilst my Mum was out with my Nana & Dad being a rubbish cook would open a packet of something to feed us. I am still a soup fiend now, both my boys are & can eat it no matter what the weather, but soup is always best on snowy, cold winter days with great big chunks of heavily buttered bread. Soup is also great for losing weight as it keeps you fuller for longer, BUT without bread of course!

Bacon & Red Lentil Soup

SERVES 4-6

This is my standby soup! It is so quick & easy to make that everyone will want to try it!

Ingredients

OO, 2 Onion, 6 Rashers of Smoked Bacon, Fresh Thyme, 300g Red Lentils, 2.5 Litres of Chicken Stock, Fresh Parmesan, Salt & Pepper.

Method

Add a glug of OO to a large pan. Finely chop the Onions & add to the pan. Roughly chop the Bacon & add to the pan & cook until the Onions & Bacon are golden. Add a small handful of Thyme Leaves, Stock & Lentils to the pan & simmer for 30 minutes. Season with Salt & Pepper, serve with lots of Fresh Parmesan grated over the top.

Curried Parsnip & Apple

SERVES 4-6

I had this soup when I was 18 years old at a restaurant for my birthday, I was shocked at the ingredients but the flavour was lovely. I recreated a few times before I got here & this is my favourite.

Ingredients

1.5 Litres of Warm Vegetable Stock, 1Kg of Parsnips, 2 Large Cooking Apples, 2 Onions, 2 Garlic Cloves, 1½ tsp. Coriander Seeds, 1½ tsp. Cumin Seeds, 50g Butter, 1 tsp. Ground Ginger, 1 tsp. Ground Turmeric, 1tsp. Cardamom Pods , Fresh Coriander, VO, 200g of Pine Nuts or Almond Flakes.

Method

Peel & Chop the Onions & Parsnips into bite sizes pieces. Set aside. Break open the Cardamom Pods & remove the seeds throwing away the husks. In a frying pan heat the Coriander, Cumin & Cardamom Seeds until they are toasted. Pour into a Pestle & Mortar & pound until crushed. Melt the Butter in a large pan & add a large glug (approx. 2 tbsp.) of VO. Add the Onions & cook until translucent. Chop the Garlic Cloves & add to the pan. Add the Toasted Spies, Ground Ginger & Turmeric. Add the Parsnips, & the Vegetable Stock. Simmer gently for 45 minutes until the Parsnips are tender. Allow to cool. Blend until smooth, & return to the heat. Season with Salt & Pepper. Peel the Apples & grate in to the pan, simmer for 5 minutes & serve. Add the Nuts to a dry pan & cook until lightly toasted. Dress with chopped Fresh Coriander & Toasted Nuts.

Summer Vegetable Soup

SERVES 4

This is so light, but remarkably filling. It's also a great way of filling the kids up with veggies.

Ingredients

6 Large Soft Red Tomatoes, 4 Yellow Tomatoes, 1 Onion, 2 Courgettes, 2 Floury Potatoes (Maris Piper or the like) 2 Garlic Cloves, 2 tbsp. of Tomato Puree, 1.2l of warm Chicken Stock, 30 Fresh Basil Leaves, 100g Parmesan, Salt & Pepper.

Method

Boil the Kettle. With a sharp knife score a cross on the bottom of each Tomato. Pour the boiled water over the Tomatoes & leave for 1 minute. Remove the Tomato skins & throw away. Finely chop the Tomatoes removing the seeds. Add a glug of OO to a large pan & add the Tomatoes. Finely chop the Onion & cook until softened. Peel & chop the Potatoes into small cubes, crush the Garlic & add to the pan. Mix well & cook for 10 minutes, stirring frequently so the Potatoes do not catch. Add the Chicken Stock & put on a low simmer for 15 minutes. Add more stock if required. Remove from the heat. Place 20 Basil Leaves on top of each other, roll up like a cigar & finely slice. Add to the pan along with 50g of grated Parmesan. Transfer into serving bowls, shave Parmesan over the top & place a few whole Basil Leaves on the top.

Tomato Soup with Pesto

SERVES 4

The Pesto takes this soup to another level. It can also be served cold as it is quite refreshing.

Ingredients

OO, 6 Large Soft Red Tomatoes, 4 Yellow Tomatoes, 1 Onion, 2 Courgettes, Floury Potatoes, 4 Garlic Cloves, 2 tbsp. of Tomato Puree, 1.2 Litres of warm Chicken Stock, 30 Basil Leaves, 100g Parmesan, 100g of Pine Nuts, Salt & Pepper.

Method

Boil the Kettle. With a sharp knife score a cross on the bottom of each Tomato. Pour the boiled water over the Tomatoes & leave for 1 minute. Remove the Tomato skins & throw away. Finely chop the Tomatoes removing the seeds. Add a glug of OO to a large pan & add the Tomatoes. Finely chop the Onion & cook until softened. Peel & chop the Potatoes into small cubes, crush 2 of the Garlic Cloves & add to the pan. Mix well & cook for 10 minutes, stirring frequently so the Potatoes do not catch. Add the Chicken Stock & put on a low simmer for 15 minutes. Add more Stock if required. Remove from the heat. Allow to cool for 20 minutes. Using a hand blender, work until smooth. Toast the Pine Nuts in a dry pan until golden. Transfer into a Food Processor & add the Basil Leaves, 2 Garlic Cloves & 100g of Grated Parmesan. Loosen with OO & blend until smooth. Place the Soup on a low heat & simmer until heated through. Transfer the Tomato Soup in to bowls, drizzle the Pesto over the top. Eat!

My Mum's Chicken & Sweetcorn Soup

SERVES 4-6

My Mum makes this all the time as my Little Boy, Ozzie loves it & we discovered that he was going to be a soup fiend just like me & Dad. Ozzie eats this with Prawn Crackers & will easily have 3-4 small Chinese style bowlfuls for lunch.

Ingredients

Carcass of a Roasted Chicken, skin removed but any flesh left on the bones, 1 tin of Sweetcorn, Corn Flour, Salt & Pepper.

Method

Place the Carcass in a large pan & cover with water. Bring to the boil & simmer for 1½ hours. Check every 30 minutes to ensure the pan does simmer dry, top up with extra water if required. Sieve the liquid into a clean pan & remove any Chicken flesh from the carcass & add to the stock. Drain the Sweetcorn & add to the stock. Cook for 5 minutes. Mix 1tbsp. of Corn Flour with a little water in a small dish. Bring the Chicken & Sweetcorn broth to the boil & add the Corn Flour, stir well as the mixture will thicken. Season with Salt & Pepper. Serve in small bowls & don't forget the Prawn Crackers.

Gazpacho – For Susie B – Because the first time I made it I made it for you xxxx

SERVES 4-6

This is so lovely & refreshing. You can make it as chunky or as smooth as you prefer. I have had it as both & have enjoyed it both ways. I think it is amazing! I also like it chunky with celery but hate it with cucumber which you could also add. If you don't like Coriander you can swap for Parsley.

Ingredients

10 Large Soft Tomatoes, 2 Garlic Cloves, 1 Onion, 2 Red Peppers, 1 Yellow Pepper, 1 Green Pepper, Red Wine Vinegar, Water, EVO, Salt & Pepper, Hot Sauce or Fresh Chillies to dress, & a Large Handful Coriander.

Method

Cut everything into bite sized chunks, setting 1/5th aside. Put the Tomatoes in a blender, add a glug of Red Wine Vinegar, a larger glug of EVO, season with Salt & Pepper. Pulse until it has reached the level you prefer, (smooth or chunky). Check the seasoning, add more Vinegar & EVO if required. Pour into a large bowl, cover & place in the fridge overnight! Before serving with warm chunky bread, adjust the seasoning again, ladle into bowls, top with the remaining veggies, thinly slice a Red & Green Chilli & sprinkle over the top or add a few slugs of your favourite hot sauce.

Chicken Ramen

SERVES 4

I have made this so many times & it is delicious. I like to make it in a great big serving bowl & let people dig in. It is great for lunch & even people who don't like soup!

Ingredients

2 litres of Chicken Stock, OO, 4 Chicken Breasts, 2 Pak Choi, 8 Spring Onions, 1 tin of Bamboo Shoots, Soy Sauce, Salt & Pepper.

Method

Coat the Chicken Breast with OO & season with Salt &

Pepper. Heat a griddle pan until smoking & then add the Chicken Breast & sear until branded & cooked on the outside. Remove from the pan & set aside. Heat the Chicken Stock, slice the Chicken Breasts on the angle & add to the Stock. Simmer the Stock until the Chicken Breast meat is cooked through. Add the Bamboo Shoots & Pak Choi leaves. Slice the Spring Onions & add to the pan. Remove the Chicken, pour into a large serving dish, top with the Chicken & place in the centre of the table & let people help themselves, with a ladle, bowl, chopsticks & a spoon.

Celeriac Soup with Bacon – For Karen WB because you said it was the "Best thing you had ever eaten"

SERVES 4

This soup is sooo creamy.

Ingredients

700g of Celeriac, 450g of Potatoes, 1.2 Litres of Warm Vegetable Stock, OO, 2 Onions, 6 Rashers of Streaky Bacon, 100g of Butter, Fresh Thyme, Fresh Rosemary, 150ml of Single Cream, 100g of Rocket Leaves, Salt & Pepper

Method

Add 50g of Butter to a large pan. Finely chop the Onions & add to the pan, cooking until translucent. Peel the Celeriac & chop into golf ball size chunks, add to the pan & cook gently for 10 minutes stirring every now & then. Peel the Potatoes & chop into similar sized chunks as the Celeriac, adding to the pan. Add the Vegetable Stock, bring to the boil & reduce to a simmer for 20 minutes. Roughly chop the Bacon, add to the pan with the Onions & cook until golden. Add a small handful of Thyme Leaves, Stock & Lentils & simmer for 30 minutes. Divide into two equal batches. Blend one half &

then return both batches to the pan. In a frying pan, melt the remaining Butter, finely chop the Bacon into thin strips & cook for 3 minutes until crispy. Finely chop the Thyme & Rosemary, add to the pan & cook for 5 minutes. Season with Salt & Pepper. Add the Cream to the Soup, stir well. Pour into bowls, top with Fresh Rocket & the Bacon & Herbs.

Roasted Pepper Soup

SERVES 4

Light, fresh & zingy!

Ingredients

2 Red Peppers, 2 Yellow Peppers, 600ml of Cold Water, 4 Garlic Cloves, OO, ½ Tin of Chopped Tomatoes, The Zest & Juice of 1 Orange, Fresh Chives, 75ml of Sour Cream, Salt & Pepper.

Method

Heat the Oven to 200°C. Chop the Peppers & remove the Seeds & Pith. Chop with the Onions roughly. Add to a large roasting tray along with the Garlic Cloves still in their skins, drizzle with OO, mix well & cook for 25-30 minutes until slightly coloured. Leave to cool. Squeeze the Garlic out of their skins & into a Blender. Add the Roasted Vegetables, Orange Juice, Orange Zest, Tinned Tomatoes, Water & blend until smooth. Pour in to a pan & heat slowly. Pour into bowls, swirl with Sour Cream & cover with chopped Chives.

Butternut Squash, Coconut & Chilli Soup – For Kate

SERVES 4

I went out for lunch with my lovely friend Kate & we popped into a little Bistro where Kate ordered this soup, it was so creamy & delicious I had to make it myself & Kate says it is exactly the same if not better! (She might be a little biased)

Ingredients

1 Large Butternut Squash, 1 Onion, OO, 1 Can of Coconut Milk, 1.2 Litres of Chicken or Vegetable Stock, 1 Red Chilli, 1 Green Chilli, Salt & Pepper.

Method

Add a glug of OO to a large pan & put on a low heat, finely chop the Onion & add to the pan, cook until soft. Season with Salt. Finely chop the Chillies, add half to the pan & reserve the rest. Cook until soft but not going brown. Peel & chop the Butternut Squash, add to the pan & stir for 5 minutes, add the stock, bring to the boil, reduce to a simmer, until the Squash is soft. Allow to cool for 20 minutes. Pour into a Blender or use a hand blender & pulse until smooth. Return to the pan, add the Coconut Milk & heat through. Pour into bowls. Finely chop the remaining Chillies if you have a taste for them & sprinkle them on the top.

Chicken & Mushroom Soup

SERVES 4

The Porcini Mushroom Liquor makes a Mushroom Ketchup which gives this soup such an earthy richness.

Ingredients

500ml of Water, 500ml of Chicken Stock, 30g of Porcini Mushrooms, 400g of Mixed Fresh Mushrooms, 2 Garlic Cloves, 1 tsp. Fresh Ginger, 2 Chicken Breasts still on the bone, ½ Lime, Fresh Parsley, Salt & Pepper.

Method

Boil the kettle. Allow to cool for 10 minutes, place the Porcini Mushrooms into a bowl & cover with the boiled water. Leave for 20 minutes. Remove the Mushrooms from the bowl, & pour almost all the liquid into a pan, not the last amount as this will contain grit. Roughly chop the Porcini. Add 1 Litre of Water to the Mushroom liquid & bring to the boil. Reduce the heat & simmer for 20 minutes until reduced by half. Slice 1/3 of the mixed Mushrooms, finely chop the Garlic & Ginger, place in a new pan with the Porcini for 3-4 minutes. Pour the liquid over the top of the Mushrooms & add the Chicken Breasts. Simmer for 15 minutes. Remove the Chicken from the pan & remove the meat. Return the bones to the pan & simmer for 30 minutes. Sieve the stock into a new pan. Bring to the boil. Cut the remaining Mushrooms into quarters, add to the pan along with the Chicken Breast Meat & the Juice of ½ a Lime. Simmer for 10 minutes. Ladle into bowls, scatter with finely chopped Fresh Parsley & enjoy.

Tuscan Bean Soup

SERVES 4

Ingredients

2 Onions, 450g of Baby Spinach, 2 Carrots, 4 Garlic Cloves, 2 Celery Sticks, 2 Courgettes, 1 Tin of Tomatoes, 1 Litre of Vegetable Stock, 1 Tin of Borlotti Beans, 2 tbsp. of Pesto, Salt & Pepper.

Method

Heat a large glug of OO in a large pan. Chop the Onions, Carrots, Garlic, Celery & Fennel & cook for 10 minutes, stirring often. Season with Salt & Pepper. Drain the Beans, add the Tomatoes, Beans & Stock to a pan & bring to the boil. Simmer for 30 minutes. Add the Pesto. Season with Salt & Pepper. Line each serving bowl with the Spinach & pour over the vegetables. Drizzle with OO & season with Pepper.

Mains Chicken

Chicken & Bacon with Tomato Sauce.

SERVES 4

Ingredients

OO, 2 Garlic Cloves, 300g of very Ripe Red Tomatoes, 75g Mascarpone Cheese, 250g Mozzarella, 1 Onion, Fresh Basil, Fresh Parsley, 1tsp. Caster Sugar, 4 Chicken Breasts, 8 slices of Prosciutto, Parmesan Cheese, Salt & Pepper.

Method

Boil the kettle. Score a cross shaped mark on the bottom of each Tomato. Cover the Tomatoes with boiling water & leave for 1 minute. Remove the skins from the Tomato, cut into quarters & remove the seeds. Roughly chop the Onion. Add a glug of OO to a large pan & add 2 Garlic Cloves, move in the pan until golden on both sides, add the Tomatoes, Onion, a large pinch of Salt, 1tsp. Caster Sugar, Pepper & cook on a low heat for 15 minutes with a lid on. Allow to cool. Blend until smooth. Add the Mascarpone & mix well. Season with Salt & Pepper. Heat the oven to 180°. Slice the Mozzarella balls into pieces. Place in the underside of the Chicken & wrap with Prosciutto. Place in an oven proof dish, pour over the sauce & cook for 30 minutes.

Chicken Ciaccatore

SERVES 4

This is a stew that is full of flavour & deliciously warming.

Ingredients

6 Chicken Breasts, 1 Onion, 2 Carrots, 2 Garlic Cloves, 2 Celery Sticks, 2tbsp. of Tomato Puree, 1 Tin of Tomatoes, 1 ½ glasses of White Wine, 500ml of Chicken Stock, 1 Stem of Rosemary, 3 Bay Leaves, Sugar, Salt & Pepper.

Method

Add a large glug of OO to a pan & place on a medium heat. Finely chop the Onions & crush the Garlic Cloves & add to the pan. Add a pinch of Salt. Turn down a low heat. Peel the Carrots & chop with the Celery & add to the pan. Cook for 5 minutes until the Onion is just starting to colour. Turn up the heat, add the Chicken & stir until the Chicken is browning. Add the Wine & simmer until the Wine is reduced by a third. Add the Tomato Puree, stir well, add the Tomatoes, Rosemary Stem, Bay Leaves & Stock. Simmer for 30 minutes. Serve with Rosemary Potatoes.

Lemony Garlic Chicken

SERVES 4

Ingredients

OO, 4 Chicken Breasts, 3 Lemons, 6 Garlic Cloves, 500g New Potatoes, Fresh Mint Leaves, Thin Green Beans, Salt & Pepper.

Method

Heat the oven to 180°C. Wash the Chicken Breasts & pat dry. Drizzle with OO & season with Salt & Pepper. Thinly slice 2 Lemons & the Garlic Cloves. Cut each of the Green Beans into 3 equal pieces. Place the Chicken, Garlic & Green Beans in an oven proof dish, add a glug of OO, the Juice of 1 Lemon, Lemon Slices & mix well. Wash & cut the New Potatoes in half, add to the dish & mix well. Cook for 35 minutes. Scatter with finely sliced Mint Leaves.

Chicken & Chorizo

SERVES 6

This is one of My Husband's favourites!

Ingredients

1 Onion, 1 Red Onion, 500g of New Potatoes, 1 Garlic Bulb, 300g Chorizo (Plain or Spicy), 6 Chicken Breasts, 1 Green Pepper, 1 Red Pepper, 10 Tomatoes, 1tsp. Smoked Paprika, 1 tsp. Dried Oregano, Salt & Pepper.

Method

Heat the Oven to 180°C. Cut the Onions into Wedges, wash & dry the Potatoes, split the Garlic Bulb into individual Cloves, but don't peel. Cut the Tomatoes into wedges, drizzle some OO into a roasting pan & add all the Vegetables. Season with Salt & Pepper, mix well. Place in the oven for 20 minutes. Cut the Chicken Breasts into 3 pieces, lightly score the meat & season. Slice the Chorizo in 3 cm chunks. Remove the

Vegetables from the oven. Add the Chicken to the roasting tin, along with the Chorizo, sprinkle the Smoked Paprika & Oregano over the ingredients & mix well. Place back in the oven for 40 minutes, after 20 minutes Slice the Peppers & add to the roasting tin. Remove from the oven every 10 minutes & collect the juices in a corner of the tin & pour over the dish. Serve immediately.

My Cyprus Chicken Kebabs
SERVES 4
This was my favourite Take Out in Cyprus. You can use Chicken or Pork. You can also cook these on a BBQ.

Ingredients
4 Large Chicken Breasts, 4 Large Pitta Breads, 1 Onion, 6 Tomatoes, a Large Handful of Parsley, OO, Lemon Juice, & Salt.

Method
Heat the grill up to its highest temperature. Cut the Chicken Breasts into small bite size pieces & thread onto a skewer. Cover a large flat oven tray with foil and place the skewers on top. Season with Salt. Finely chop the Onion & cut the Tomatoes into small cubes. Cook the Chicken until the meat starts to char & rotate the skewer until all the Chicken is fully cooked. Remove from the Grill. Place the Pitta breads until the grill & cook on each side until they start to colour & puff up. Fill each Pitta with a skewer of Meat, Onion, Tomato & Parsley. Dress with Salt, OO & Lemon Juice. Serve with Tashi (Dashi) Dip.

Spicy Rubbed Chicken

SERVES 4

The greatest thing about this dish is that you make the rub in a large quantity & store in an airtight tub, it will keep for weeks so if you want to make it again quickly it's ready for you – All you need is Chicken.

Ingredients

4 Chicken Breast, OO, Salt & Pepper. (For the Rub – Make this & place in an air tight container where it will keep for months. You can halve the quantities.) 4 tbsp. of Smoked Paprika, 1 tbsp. of Cayenne Pepper, 5 tbsp. of Ground Cumin, 2 tbsp. Dried Thyme, 2tbsp. Dried Oregano, 2 tbsp. Ground Black Pepper & 1 tbsp. of Sea Salt.

Method

Put all the rub ingredients into a sealable bag. Wash the Chicken Breasts & pat dry. Lightly score the Chicken. Add the Chicken to the sealable bag, shake well & smoosh so the pub gets into all the grooves. Place in the fridge for a couple of hours. Heat the oven to 200°C. Remove the Chicken from the bag & shake off any excess, drizzle lightly with OO. Place in the oven for 25 minutes until the Chicken is cooked.

Chicken Korma (ish)

SERVES 4

This is so mild, silky & creamy. If you want to spice it up add more Chilli Powder. The Cardamom really sets this off & I love smelling the spices as they cook.

Ingredients

4 Chicken Breasts, A large tub of Greek Yoghurt, SFO, 2 Onions, 4 Garlic Cloves, Red Chillies, 30g of Fresh Ginger, 4tbsp. of Fresh Ginger, 16 Cardamom Pods, 1tsp. of Cumin

Seeds, 1tsp. Ground Coriander, 10 Strands of Saffron, 5 Clove Heads, ½ Turmeric Powder, 2 Bay Leaves, A Small Handful of Raisins, ½ – 1 tsp. Hot Chilli Powder (depending on your taste) 1 tin of Coconut Milk, 1 tsp. of Caster Sugar, 1 tbsp. of Plain Flour, 100ml of Double Cream, Sliced Almonds, Salt & Pepper.

Method

Cut the Chicken up into medium sized chunks. Place in a ceramic bowl, cover with Greek Yoghurt, wrap & place in the fridge for at least 2 hours, you can do this in the morning & then the rest in the evening. Chop the Onions, Garlic & Ginger. Add a glug of SFO to a large deep pan. Add the Onions, Garlic & Ginger & cook slowly until golden. Open the Cardamom Pods & remove the seeds. Put the Cumin Seeds in a Pestle & Mortar & crush, add the Cardamom Seeds & repeat. Add the Ground Coriander, Turmeric, & Chilli Powder, pull off the Clove Heads, add & mix well. Add to the pan & stir whilst cooking for 5 minutes. Add a tbsp. of Plain Flour, Saffron, 2 Bay Leaves, a tbsp. of Caster Sugar, a pinch of Salt & just cover with Cold Water. Simmer gently for 10 minutes. Remove the Bay Leaves, allow to cool & blend until smooth. Return to the pan, cook on a low heat & add the Chicken Pieces from the yoghurt. Pour the Coconut Cream into a jug, stir well & add to the pan. Cook the Chicken through, add the cream & season with Salt & Pepper.

Add the Almonds to a dry pan, & cook until toasted. Garnish the Korma with Fresh Coriander & the Almonds. I serve with Lemongrass & Coriander Rice.

Chicken Chow Mein

SERVES 4

A brilliant "Fake Away"

Ingredients

2 Chicken Breasts, 3 Garlic Cloves, 250g Sugar Snap Peas, 3 Spring Onions, 1 Carrot, 500g of Medium Egg Noodles, Fresh or Dried, 1 tbsp. of Sesame Oil, 3 tbsp. of Dry Sherry, 2 tbsp. of Groundnut or VO, 2 tbsp. of Light & Dark Soy Sauce, Salt & Pepper.

Method

Cook the Noodles as per the instructions on the packet. Once cooked, drain, place in a bowl & cover with the Sesame Oil, toss & set aside. Finely chop the Garlic Cloves & cut the Chicken into small bite size pieces. Heat the oil in a large frying pan or a wok if you have one, & once it starts to smoke add the Garlic & stir for about 30 seconds, then add the Chicken. Stir well so the Chicken doesn't catch. Add the Sugar Snap Peas & mix well. Add the Sherry & leave to reduce for about 5 minutes. Add the Soy Sauces & a pinch of Salt & Pepper. Finely slice the Spring Onion & Carrots in to matchsticks, add to the pan, stir well & leave for 3 minutes or so. Spoon into bowls & eat!

Smoked Paprika Chicken

SERVES 4

Easy 1 pan dinner.

Ingredients

OO, 6 Chicken Breasts, 2 Red Peppers, 2 Yellow Peppers, 2 Medium Onions, 2 Garlic Cloves, 2 tbsp. Smoked Paprika, 1 Tin of Chopped Tomatoes, 500 ml of Chicken Stock, 2 Bay Leaves, 1 tbsp. of Mixed Dried Herbs, Thick Natural Greek

Yoghurt, Corn Flour, Salt & Pepper.

Method

Heat the oven to 180°C. Add the OO to a pan. Chop the Onions in half & then cut into slices. Add to the pan & cook until soft & just starting to colour. Cut the Chicken Breasts into quarters, season with Salt & Pepper & add to the pan. Cook until coloured. Thinly slice the Garlic, add to the pan along with the Paprika & stir for one minute. Add the Tomatoes, Chicken Stock, Bay Leaves & Herbs to the pan & bring to the boil, reducing to a simmer for 20 minutes. Slice the Peppers removing the seeds. Add to the pan. Place in the oven 40 minutes, stir after 20 minutes. Remove from the oven & put back on the hob on a low heat. Add a little Corn Flour to a bowl & mix with water into a paste, add to the pan & stir until thickened. Serve with Pourgori.

Greek Chicken with Roast Baby Potatoes

SERVES 4

Probably one of my favourite Chicken Dishes but definitely my little one's favourite Potatoes.

Ingredients

500g of Baby Potatoes, 1 Onion, 8 Large Boneless & Skinless Chicken Thighs, 5 Garlic Cloves, 1 tin of Chopped Tomatoes, 20 Black Pitted Olives, 1tbsp. of Fresh Thyme Leaves, 2 tbsp. of Fresh Oregano Leaves, 3tbsp. of Dried Mixed Herbs, OO, Salt & Pepper.

Method

Put a large pan of salted water on to boil & add the washed Potatoes in their skins. Bring to the boil & reduce to a low simmer for 10 minutes. Take off the heat, put the pan in the sink & fill the pan with Cold Water. Set aside to cool. Heat the Oven to 180°C. Add a glug of OO to a large deep pan &

sear all the Chicken Thighs in batches. Leave aside on a plate. Chop the Onion & 2 of the Garlic Cloves & add to the pan with a little more OO & cook until the Onion is translucent. Add the Tomatoes, Olives, Oregano, Thyme, & season with Salt & Pepper. Add the Chicken Thighs & place in the middle of the oven for 25-30 minutes. Smash the remaining 3 Garlic Cloves in a Pestle & Mortar, add a little Salt & smooth round the dish. Add the Dried Mixed Herbs, mix again & add OO until it becomes a very loose mixture. Drizzle OO onto a large roasting tray, add the potatoes, shake on the tray & spoon the Garlic & Herb mixture over the Potatoes & shake again. Place in the top of the oven for 25-30 minutes. It's Gorgeous.

Sticky Chicken

SERVES 4

Ingredients

4 Chicken Breast, 4 Long Red Chillies, 30g of Fresh Ginger, 4tbsp. Fish Sauce, 150ml of White Wine Vinegar, 2 Lemongrass Stalks, 150g Caster Sugar, Salt & Pepper.

Method

Finely slice the Chillies & remove the seeds (unless you like things very spicy). Peel the Ginger & finely grate. Finely chop the white part of the Lemongrass. Place the Chillies, Ginger, Lemongrass, Fish Sauce, White Wine Vinegar & Sugar in a shallow frying pan & bring to the boil, reduce to a simmer until reduced. Keep stirring as it will catch if you leave it. Add the Chicken & cook for 4-5 minutes on each side. Serve with plain White Rice & Mange Tout.

Beef

Gorgeous Burgers

<u>SERVES 4</u>

I've made different types of burgers & these stand out by far.

<u>Ingredients</u>

OO, 500g of Beef Mince, 2 Garlic Cloves, 2 Mozzarella Balls, ½ Red Onion, 100g of Fresh Breadcrumbs, Rocket Leaves, 2 Beef Tomatoes, 4 Soft Bread Rolls, Salt & Pepper.

<u>Method</u>

Finely chop the Garlic. Place in a bowl & add the Beef & Breadcrumbs. Season with Salt & Pepper. Make into flat rounds, about 3cm deep, place on a plate, cover with cling film & place in the fridge until ready to cook. Heat a griddle pan until smoking. Cook the Burgers for 4 minutes each side or longer if you prefer. Remove from the griddle. Cover the base of the Bread Roll with Rocket Leaves & top with a Burger, a slice of Mozzarella, Tomato & Red Onion.

Lasagne

SERVES 4

My secret to a brilliant Lasagne is to leave it overnight to let all the flavours develop. If you make the Red Sauce in **Sides** you only need to fry the Onion, Herbs, add the Meat & Stock.

Ingredients

OO, 500g of Beef Mince, 2 Garlic Cloves, 1 Large Onion, Dried Italian Herbs, 1 glass of Red Wine, 10 White & 10 Brown Mushrooms, 2 tins of Chopped Tomatoes, 2 x Beef Stock Cubes, Sugar, Salt & Pepper, 75g of Butter, 150g of Plain Flour, 1 Litre of room temperature Full Cream Milk, Salt & Pepper, 100g of Cheddar, Grated Mozzarella & Parmesan Cheese.

Method

Finely chop the Onion, add a glug of OO to a large deep pan & slowly cook the Onion until soft. Add 1 tbsp. of Italian Herbs & mix well, allow to cook for 2 minutes. Smash the Garlic & add to the Pan. Add the Beef & break up so there are no large chunks, add the Red Wine & simmer for 10 minutes until most of the Wine has evaporated & the Meat is cooked. Cut the Mushrooms into small pieces & add to the pan, stirring well. Add the Tomatoes, Stock Cubes, a good pinch of Sugar, season with Salt & Pepper, bring to the boil & reduce to a simmer for 30 minutes, stirring occasionally but making sure it doesn't catch. Make the **WHITE SAUCE** by slowly melting the Butter in a pan, add the Flour. Keep stirring, this will go lumpy but you have to cook the taste of the Flour out. Use a wooden spoon for this. This takes a couple of minutes. Turn up to a medium heat. Slowly add the Milk, stirring the Butter & Flour with the wooden spoon. Change to using a whisk once there is liquid in the pan. Slowly, slowly keep adding the Milk. Once the Milk has thickened to a creamy consistency you can stop adding the Milk. Season with Salt & Pepper. Add one large serving spoonful of the Meat Mixture to a Lasagne dish, cover with Lasagne Sheets, top with the Meat Mixture, cover with Lasagne Sheets, top with White Sauce, cover with Lasagne sheets & repeat until all of the Meat Mixture is used & finish with a layer of the White Sauce. Add more grated Cheese if you wish. Cook at 180°C for 30 minutes until golden & bubbling.

Stifado

SERVES 4

I look forward to the winter cold days when I can eat fantastic stews & this is one of them. Total comfort food.

Ingredients

OO, 1kg Stewing Steak, 500g of Shallots, 500g of Baby Vine Tomatoes, 4 Garlic Cloves, 3 Bay Leaves,1 Litre of Hot Beef Stock, 1 Cinnamon Stick, 2 glasses Red wine, 1-2 of Red Wine Vinegar, 2 Clove Heads, 2-3 Bay leaves, Tomato Puree, Fresh Rosemary, Salt & Pepper.

Method

Finely chop the Shallots & Garlic Cloves. Add a glug of OO to a large deep pan, heat gently, add the Meat & cook until browned on all sides. Add the Shallots & cook until softened & add the garlic. Pour in the Red Wine & the Vinegar. Cover with a lid & simmer for 5 minutes. Add the Bay Leaves, Cinnamon & Cloves & mix well. Add the

Tomatoes, mix well & add the Tomato Puree, stir in & cook for 2 minutes. Add enough Beef Stock to cover the ingredients & bring to the boil. Reduce to a low simmer & cover with the lid. Cook until the liquid is reduced & the Meat is tender which should be approximately 2 hours. Stir often. Add more stock if required.

Beef Stroganoff

SERVES 4

Steak, Mushrooms & Cream! Need I say more?

Ingredients

OO, 500g of Fillet Steak, 300g of Chestnut Mushrooms, 1 Onion, 250ml of Beef Stock, 50ml of Brandy, 2tbsp. Horseradish Sauce, 200ml of Soured Cream, Salt & Pepper.

Method

Roughly chop the Onion & cut the Mushrooms into quarters. Add a glug of OO to a large pan & add the Mushrooms & cook until just softened. Add the Onions to the pan & cook until turning brown in colour. Slice the Beef into thin strips & add to the pan until just turning in colour, add the Brandy & set light to it. Once the flames have gone out add ¾ of the Soured Cream & the Horseradish Sauce. Season with Salt & Pepper & serve immediately.

A Shepherd who lived in a Cottage (Pie)

SERVES 4-6

I always make my Shepherd's Pie with Beef, although traditionally it is Cottage Pie that is made with Beef & Shepherd's Pie that is made with Lamb, so this is my Shepherd who lived in A Cottage Pie. Made with Beef.

Ingredients

OO, 500g of Aberdeen Angus Minced Beef, 1 Large Onion, 250g of White & Chestnut Mushrooms (Total), 750ml of Beef Stock, 2 Beef Stock Cubes, 1 Large Glass of Red Wine, 1 Small Swede, 3 Carrots, 100g of Frozen Peas, 1Kg of White Floury Potatoes, 75g of Butter, 100g of Cheddar Cheese, 1 Large Tomato, 1tsp. Corn Flour, Salt & Pepper.

Method

Roughly chop the Onion. Cut the Mushrooms in to quarters. Peel the Swede & cut into small chunks & do the same with the Carrots. Add a glug of OO to a large frying pan & add the Onion, cook until softened. Add the Meat & break up. Add the Wine & simmer until reduced. Add the Carrot, Swede & Mushrooms & mix in well. Add the Beef Stock & Stock Cubes. Season well & allow to simmer for 30 minutes. Peel the Potatoes & cut into golf ball size pieces. Place in a pan of salted boiled water & simmer until tender. Add the Frozen Peas to the Meat, stir in & cook for 2 minutes. Drain the Meat, reserving the liquid. Transfer the Meat into a large oven proof dish. Mash the Potatoes, with Butter, (DO NOT ADD MILK, this will make the Potato sink). Top the Meat with the Potatoes, run a fork up & down the length of the dish to make a pattern & cover with Grated Cheddar Cheese. Top with slices of Tomato. Place in the oven for 25 minutes at 180°C until the Cheese is bubbling & golden. Return the Meat Liquid to a clean saucepan, bring to the boil, mix the Corn Flour with water & add to the liquid so it thickens. Fabulous!

Pork

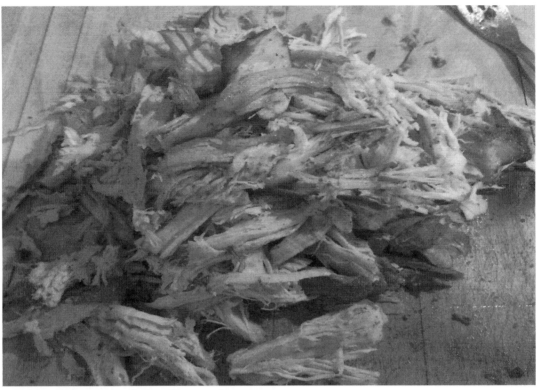

Belly Pork with Port & Soy

SERVES 4-6

This is a joy to eat. It does take some preparation the night before but it is so delicious it is definitely worth it.

Ingredients

1Kg piece of Belly Pork, 150ml Soy Sauce, 500ml of Port, 150g of Light Brown Sugar, 150ml of Dry Sherry, 200ml of Runny Honey, 3 Red Onions, 2 Celery Sticks, 2 Large Carrots, 6 Coriander Seeds, 6 Peppercorns, 2 Bay Leaves, 3 Sprigs of Fresh Thyme, 3 Star Anise, Salt & Pepper.

Method

Wash the Pork & dry with some Kitchen Roll. Chop the

Onions, Celery & Carrots. Pour the Port, Soy, & Honey into a large bowl. Add the Carrots, Celery & Onions, Sugar, Spices & Thyme & mix well. Add the Pork making sure it is completely covered, cover with cling film & leave in the fridge overnight. Heat the Oven to 160°C. Remove the Pork from the marinade, remove any vegetables from it. Pass the marinade through a sieve, reserving the vegetables & transfer to a large pan (that has a lid & can go in the oven), bring to the boil & simmer until it has reduced by half. Allow to cool. Add the Pork to the marinade, cover it well, add the vegetables again & cook in the oven for 3 hours, checking every 30 minutes or so to make sure the liquid has not evaporated. Allow to cool for a while, remove the Pork from the pan, sieve the liquid again, discard the Vegetables & return to a pan until reduced further. Slice the Pork & pour over the sauce. Serve with Spinach & gorgeous Mashed Potato.

Maple Syrup Pulled Pork – For Karen M who lets me take over her kitchen & eats everything I make with the biggest smile on her face!! xxx

SERVES 4-6

This is a treat & a half!! Perfect for large get-togethers, & for making you the most popular person in the room! I would recommend using twice the quantity as it seems that one roll is never enough!

Ingredients

1kg Pork Shoulder, 1 Onion, 2 Garlic Cloves, 1 tin of Chopped Tomatoes, 250ml Maple Syrup, 100ml Cider Vinegar, 2 tbsp. Tomato Puree, 1tbsp. Ground Coriander, 1tbsp. Ground Cinnamon, 1 tbsp. Smoked Paprika, 1 tbsp.

Ground Cumin, 50ml of Water, 75g of Soft Brown Sugar, OO, Salt & Pepper.

Method

Heat the oven to 220°C. Finely chop the Onion & the Garlic. Add a glug of OO to large pan & add the Onion & cook until just softening. Add the Garlic, Coriander, Cinnamon, Smoked Paprika, Cumin & stir well to combine. Add 50ml of Water to make a kind of paste. Add the Tomato Puree & cook for 2 minutes. Add the Vinegar, Tomatoes, Sugar & mix well. Add the Maple Syrup & cook for 30 minutes, stirring often. Score the Pork & rub with Salt & Pepper. Sear each side on a griddle pan or a frying pan for 5 minutes. Place the Pork in a deep roasting Tin & pour the Maple Syrup mixture over the top of the Pork. Place the Pork in the Oven for 30 minutes. Remove from the oven, cover the whole tray with tin foil, turn the oven down to 160°C & cook for 3 hours. Baste every 30 minutes. Once the Pork is cooked remove from the oven & allow to cool for ½ an hour. Remove the foil & using 2 forks pull the Pork apart. Serve on soft rolls with My Mum's Coleslaw.

Sweetest Sour Pork

SERVES 4

This is wonderful served as an alternative Roast Dinner with all the usual trimmings

Ingredients

OO, 2.5Kg Boneless Pork Loin, 125g of Pancetta, 125g Chestnut Mushrooms, 1 Pack of Porcini Mushrooms, 2 Garlic Cloves, 3tbsp. of Balsamic Vinegar, 2 tsp. of Dark Soft Sugar, Fresh Parsley, Salt & Pepper.

Method

Heat the Oven to 180°C. Cover the Pork in OO & Season with Salt & Pepper. Place in a roasting tin & cook for 2 & ½ hours. Remove from the tin once cooked, wrap in foil & set aside. Separate the juices & fat from the roasting tin. Pour the juices into a jug & reserve the fat. Boil the kettle. Add the Porcini Mushrooms to a bowl & cover with the boiled water. Pour half of the Pork fat into a frying pan & add the Pancetta (chop into small pieces if it isn't already) & fry until golden. Crush the Garlic Cloves & add to the pan. Allow to sit for 15 minutes. Remove the Porcini Mushrooms from the water & reserve the liquid, roughly chop & add to the pan. Add 3tbsp. of Balsamic Vinegar & the Sugar. Mix well. Add the Pork Juices & heat through. Remove any Crackling from the Pork & slice the meat. Eat & enjoy!

Aubergine with Mozzarella & Prosciutto
SERVES 4 – 6

I ordered this in Italy by mistake not realising what it was, however I was wonderfully surprised & I make this often either as a starter or as a main course with a salad. Everyone loves it, along with my Red Sauce which took a few weeks to perfect.

Ingredients
OO, 2 Aubergines, 4 Mozzarella Balls, 12 Slices of Prosciutto, **Red Sauce**, 200g Grated Parmesan, Salt & Pepper.

Method
Heat the Oven to 180°C. Make the **Red Sauce** in Sides & leave overnight if possible. Slice the Aubergines into rounds & sprinkle with a little Salt on each side. Place on kitchen roll & leave for an hour or so. Drizzle the Aubergine with OO, & place in a hot frying pan in batches until slightly coloured. Place on a plate & set aside. Lie a layer of Aubergine in a

large casserole dish. Open the Mozzarella & drain off the liquid. Chop into small pieces & scatter a thin layer over the top of the Aubergine. Cover with slices of Prosciutto & repeat. There should be 2 layers of each. Cover the top layer with 3– 4 ladles full of **Red Sauce**, cover with grated Parmesan & bake in the oven for 30 minutes until golden brown.

Chorizo in Red Wine

SERVES 4

This is a great starter or I serve with lots of other little dishes.

Ingredients

200g of Chorizo, 200ml of Good Red Wine, 2 tbsp. of Brandy, Fresh Parsley.

Method

Using a fork prick the Chorizo several times along the sausage each side. Place into a pan & cover with the Wine. Bring to the boil, reduce & simmer for 20 minutes. Allow to cool, transfer both the Chorizo & the Wine into a bowl & leave overnight to marinate. Remove the Chorizo from the Wine, but do not throw it away. Slice the Chorizo into slices about 5mm thick. Heat a frying pan & add the Chorizo & the Brandy, shake well & add the remaining Wine. Simmer on a high heat until the Wine has completely reduced. Sprinkle with chopped Fresh Parsley. Serve with Olive Bread.

Lamb

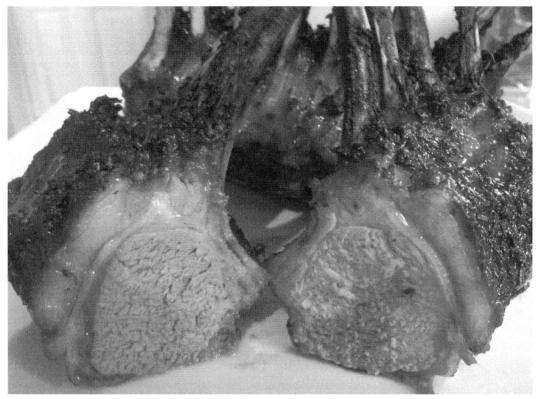

Spicy Lamb with Mango

SERVES 4

Ingredients

OO, 8 Lamb Chops, 2 Onions, 2 Mangos, 1 tsp. of Cumin Seeds, 2 tbsp. Coriander Seeds, ½ tsp. Cayenne pepper, 2 tbsp. Coarse Grain Mustard, 400ml of Natural Greek Yoghurt, Fresh Parsley, Fresh Mint, Lemon Juice, Salt & Pepper.

Method

Add a glug of OO to a frying pan. Finely chop the Onion, add a pinch of Salt & cook until translucent. Leave to cool. Gently crush the Cumin & Coriander Seeds add to a bowl along with the Mustard, Cayenne & season with Salt & Pepper. Add 200ml of Yoghurt & mix well. Add the Lamb Chop & leave for at least 2 hours or longer if you can. Heat the Grill to

200°C. Peel the Mango & roughly chop the flesh into chunks, add the remaining Yoghurt, finely chop with Fresh Parsley & Mint & add 1tbsp. of each, add 2tbsp. of Lemon Juice & adjust the seasoning with Salt & Pepper. Transfer into a small bowl. Cook the Chops to your liking, 3 minutes for me as I like rare, add a minute for medium & 2 minutes for well done. Serve with Potatoes of your choice.

Italian Lamb

SERVES 4

A gorgeous stew with a Leg of Lamb which is even tastier the following day. The meat will fall off the bone it is so tender.

Ingredients

OO, 2.5Kg Leg of Lamb, 1 Onion, 6 Carrots, 6 Celery Sticks, 125g of Porcini Mushrooms, 125g Chestnut Mushrooms, 10 Sundried Tomatoes, 400g of Passata, 150g of Thick Sliced Salami, 1 Bottle of good Italian Red Wine, 600ml of Warm Vegetable Stock, Parmesan Cheese, Fresh Parsley, Salt & Pepper.

Method

Heat the oven to 230°C. Wash the Lamb, pat dry & place in a Roasting tray. Drizzle with OO, season with Salt, Pepper & cook for 30 minutes. Boil the kettle. Allow to cool a little & add the Porcini Mushrooms to a bowl & cover with the boiled water. Leave for 15 minutes. Melt the Butter in a pan, add a small glug of OO. Finely chop the Onion, Carrots & Celery & add to the pan. Sauté for 10 minutes until soft & just coloured. Cut the Chestnut Mushrooms into quarters & remove the Porcini Mushrooms from the water, squeeze well & roughly chop. Add to the pan & cook for 5 minutes. Add the Tomatoes, Salami, Wine, Passata & Vegetable stock, bring to the boil, reduce to a simmer & cook for 10 minutes. Remove the Lamb from the oven & set aside. Lift the Lamb & pour the Tomato mix into the Roasting Tray, place the Lamb on top, cover with foil, reduce the heat to 160°C & cook for 3 hours. Check after 2 hours, & return to the oven for another hour. Remove from the Oven, remove the Lamb & set aside. Pour the Tomato mix back into a pan, bring to the boil, reduce to a simmer add 25g of grated Parmesan & stir well. Slowly cook for 10 minutes. Place the Lamb on a Serving Dish & pour the Tomato Sauce over the top. Finely chop the Parsley & scatter with some extra Parmesan.

Kleftico

SERVES 4

I used to eat this all the time at a restaurant by the Beach. It was cooked in a clay oven but you can almost get the same results in a normal oven. The key is slowly, slowly. Buy the Lamb & ask your Butcher to cut the Lamb into 5cm pieces.

Ingredients

2kg Leg of Lamb, 8 Potatoes, 750ml of Lamb or Beef Stock, 2-3 Bay Leaves & 1tbsp. of Oregano.

Method

Heat the Oven to 180°C. Place the Lamb Pieces in a large Casserole Dish or Pan with a lid. Add the Stock, the Bay Leaves & the Oregano. Cover with a lid & place in the oven for 1 hour. Peel the Potatoes & slice length ways. Add to the Lamb. Cook until the Meat can be pulled from the bone & the Potatoes are soft & tender. If you need more water add to the pan (but only use hot boiled water).

Lamb & Potato Curry

SERVES 4

Ingredients

OO, 4-6 Lamb Steaks, 450g of Potatoes, 2 Onions, 4 Fresh Tomatoes, 1 pack of Baby Spinach Leaves, 1 tin of Chopped Tomatoes, 4 Garlic Cloves, a thumb sized piece of Ginger, 1 (or 2) Red Chillies, 75g of Curry Paste, 2 Bay Leaves, Fresh Greek Yogurt, Sugar, Salt & Pepper.

Method

Cut the Lamb into large chunks, coat with OO & season with Salt & Pepper. Place in a large frying pan & sear on all sides. Remove to a plate & set aside. Chop the Onions, & add to a pan with a glug of OO & cook for 5 minutes until they are soft & just turning in colour. Add the Garlic Cloves, Ginger & Chillies & add to the pan along with the Curry Paste & cook for another 5 minutes. (Choose a Curry paste that suits your palate, mild, medium or hot) Allow to cool & transfer to a blender or use a handheld one blending together until smooth. Return to the pan on a low heat & add the Lamb. Heat the oven to 180°C. Peel the Potatoes & cut into large golf ball sized pieces. Add the Tinned Tomatoes, Potatoes, Bay Leaves, a large pinch of Salt, Sugar & 500ml of Water. Mix well & transfer into a Casserole Dish & place in the oven for 1 & ½ hours. Remove from Oven & cut the Fresh Tomatoes into quarters, add to the dish along with the Baby Spinach Leaves & serve with Basmati Rice & Fresh Greek Yoghurt.

Moussaka

SERVES 4-6

I really like Moussaka, it's a real change from Lasagne & it love it with salad & red wine of course.

Ingredients

OO, 600g Lamb Mince, 1 Aubergine, 2 Garlic Cloves, 1 tin of Tomatoes, 2 Bay Leaves, 1tsp. Ground Cumin, 1tsp. Ground Coriander, 1tsp. Ground Cinnamon, 1tbsp. of Tomato Puree, 1tsp. Dried Thyme, 1tsp. Dried Oregano, Salt & Pepper. **White Sauce,** 250ml Whole Milk, 25g Butter, 25g Plain Flour, a pinch of Nutmeg, 30g of Parmesan, 250g Ricotta Cheese, & 1 Egg.

Method

Heat the oven to 180°C. Slice the Aubergine into thin slices lengthways. Lie the Aubergine on kitchen roll & sprinkle each side with a little salt & leave for about 30 minutes. Rinse well & pat dry. Drizzle with OO, & add to a roasting tin & place in the oven for 30 minutes. Add a glug of OO to a large frying pan & finely chop the Garlic. Add to the pan along with the Lamb Mince & cook until browned, break the Lamb into small pieces. Add the Cayenne, Cumin, Cinnamon & Coriander, stir for 1-2 minutes. Add Herbs, Tomatoes, Tomato Puree & stir well. Reduce the heat to a low simmer & cover for 30 minutes, stirring occasionally so the mix doesn't catch. Make the White Sauce with Cheese. Melt the Butter in a pan, add the Flour & mix well. Cook out the Flour taste & slowly add the Milk until the desired thickness is achieved. Season with Salt, Pepper, grate the Parmesan & add to the pan. Leave to cool. In an oven proof dish spoon a layer of the Lamb, top with a layer of Aubergine & repeat finishing with the Lamb. Crack & beat the egg in in a bowl & add the white sauce. Pour over the Moussaka & bake in the oven for 45minutes at 180°C until golden brown. Allow to cool for 20 minutes & then serve. (I like to leave in the oven night so the flavours develop even further)

Fish

Roasted Cod with Lime

SERVES 4

Ingredients

OO, 4 Cod Fillets, 3 Garlic Cloves, 3 Pickled Jalapenos, 1 Onion, 1 Lemon, 2 Limes, a Large Handful Fresh Coriander, Salt & Pepper.

Method

Place the Cod Fillets on a large plate & season with Salt & Pepper. Cut the Limes & squeeze over the Fish. Heat a glug of OO. Finely chop the Onion & Garlic Cloves & add the pan, cooking until soft. Heat the oven 180°C. Add 1/3 of the Onion & Garlic to the bottom of an ovenproof dish. Finely chop the Jalapenos & Coriander. Add half to the dish. Place the Fish on top & cover with the remaining Onions, Garlic,

Jalapenos & Coriander. Place in the oven for 15 minutes until the Fish is firm. Serve with Lemon & Lime wedges.

Crab stuffed Mushrooms

SERVES 4

Ingredients

200g of White Crab Meat, 450g of Portobello Mushrooms, 5 Spring Onions, 2tbsp. of Mayo, ½tsp. Fresh Thyme Leaves, ½tsp. of Fresh Oregano Leaves, ½tsp. Fresh small Mint Leaves, 150g of Parmesan, ½tsp. of Paprika, Salt & Pepper.

Method

Heat the oven to 180°C. Chop the Spring Onions & finely chop the Herbs. Add the Crab Meat to a large bowl & add the Spring Onions, Herbs & Mayo. Grate the Parmesan & add a third to the bowl & mix well. Season with Pepper & place in the fridge. Wipe the Mushrooms with damp kitchen roll & remove the stems & the gills. Fill each Mushroom with the Crab Mix, sprinkle with Parmesan & Paprika. Cook in the oven for 15 minutes.

Squid with Chorizo

SERVES 2-4

Ingredients

400g of clean Squid Hoods, 12 Cherry Tomatoes, 1 Red Chilli, 3 Garlic Cloves, 75g of Chorizo, Juice of a Lemon, 100g of Chickpeas, 20g Rocket & Watercress.

Method

Wash the Squid Hoods, pat dry & lie on a chopping board. Put your knife into the Hood & slice outwards, cutting the Hoods in half, giving you two pieces. Place skin side up on the board & lightly score in a fine crisscross pattern, set aside.

Cut the Chorizo into thin slices on an angle. Drain & wash the Chickpeas. Chop the Tomatoes into quarters & add to a bowl with the Chickpeas. Add 50ml of Lemon Juice & a glug of OO to the bowl. Mix well. Finely chop the Chilli, Garlic & Parsley & add to the bowl. Season with Salt & Pepper. Add 1tbsp. of OO to a frying pan & add the Squid in two batches frying for 30 seconds on each side until golden. Return to the pan with the Chorizo & cook for 1 minute. Place the Rocket Leaves on each plate, top with the Chickpeas & place the Squid & Chorizo on top.

Prawn Cakes with Chilli & Lime

SERVES 4

Ingredients

600g Raw Tiger Prawns, 2 Spring Onions, 3 tbsp. of Mayonnaise, 2 Red Chillies, Zest & Juice of a Lime, 1 egg, 2tbsp. Fresh Coriander, 200g of Breadcrumbs, Salt & Pepper.

Method

Peel, de-vein & finely chop the Prawns. Finely chop the Chillies & Spring Onions. Zest & juice the Lime & chop the Coriander. Place the Prawns, Chillies, Spring Onions, Lime & Coriander in a bowl & mix well. Beat an egg in a different bowl & add to the mix. Add the Mayo & mix well. Take the mixture & make into balls in your hands. Place on greaseproof paper & put in fridge for 2 hours. Pour the Breadcrumbs onto a large plate. Roll the Prawn Balls in the Breadcrumbs until they are completely covered. Shallow fry in SO until golden brown & place on kitchen paper to absorb any excess oil.

Louvi

SERVES 4

This is a fantastic lunch, eaten in CY all the time. Everyone loves it, talks about it & how their Yai Yai's (Grandmother) is better than anyone else's. You can eat this hot or cold, I prefer it hot. Its better when you dress it on the plate rather than in the serving bowl, so if there is anything leftover it won't wilt in the dressing overnight.

Ingredients

EVO, 4 Tuna Steaks, 1 Bag of Spinach Leaves, 800g of Black Eyed Beans, 2 Celery Sticks, 4 Tomatoes, 1 tin of Sweetcorn, ½ a Cucumber, 1 Red Pepper, 1 Yellow Pepper, Lemon Juice, Salt & Pepper.

Method

Chop all of the vegetables & place in a serving bowl. Mix well. Wash & Drain the Beans, add to a pan & cover with water. Bring to the boil & reduce to a simmer. Cook for 5 minutes. Drizzle the Tuna Steaks with OO & season with Salt & Pepper. Heat up a Griddle Pan & cook the Tuna for 2 minutes on each side. Remove from the heat & allow to rest for a few minutes. Add the Spinach Leaves to the Beans & stir well. Drain the Beans. Add to the Vegetables. Mix well. Spoon the Beans & Vegetables onto plates. Season with Salt, add Lemon Juice & OO. Place the Tuna Steak on top. Drizzle with OO, Lemon Juice & Salt. Eat immediately.

Duck

Duck with Raspberry Sauce

SERVES 4

Ingredients

4 Duck Breasts, 100g of Raspberries, 25ml of Crème De Cassis, 100ml of Red Wine, 1tsp. of Cinnamon, 2tsp. of Salt, 1 ½tbsp of Soft Brown Sugar & Corn Flour.

Method

Use a knife to score the Duck Breasts through the skin & fat but not the meat. Heat a large frying pan on medium high. Cook the Duck Breasts skin down, until the skin browns & fat is released, about 10 minutes. Remove the Duck from the pan, & pour away nearly all the fat. In a small bowl add the Sea Salt, Sugar & Cinnamon together & sprinkle over the duck skin. Place the Duck back in the pan, & cook meat side down 10 minutes, or until desired. Sprinkle the skin with more of the sugar mix, & cook for a further minute, remove from the pan & allow to rest. Mix together the Red Wine, Crème de Cassis & 1 tsp. of Corn Flour in a small bowl. Add to the frying pan & cook for 3 minutes, stirring constantly, until the sauce has thickened. Add Raspberries, & simmer for another minute until heated through. Slice the Duck Breasts thinly, pour a little sauce over the top, & serve.

Honey Roast Duck

Ingredients

1.5Kg of Whole Duck, Fresh Thyme, Bay Leaves, 4tbsp. of Honey, Salt & Pepper.

Method

Heat oven to 220°C. Wash the Duck & pat dry with kitchen & season all over with Salt. Put a few sprigs of Thyme & the Bay Leaves inside the Duck & place on a rack over a roasting tin. Cook for 10 mins or until the skin begins to turn golden, then reduce the heat to 180°C. Cook for a further 45 mins, basting the bird with Honey every 5 mins or so for the last 20 mins. Set aside to rest, for 10 mins, carve & serve.

Slow Cooked Duck Legs with a Red Wine & Mushroom Sauce

SERVES 4

Ingredients

4 Duck Legs, 500ml of Cabernet Sauvignon Wine, 900ml of Warm Chicken Stock, 1 Large Onion, 1 Large Carrot, 2 Garlic Cloves, a few sprigs of Thyme, 2 Bay Leaves, 2tbsp. of Plain

Flour, 2 Large Portobello Mushrooms, 4 Rashers of Streaky Bacon, Salt & Pepper.

Method

Heat the Oven to 180°C. Season the Duck with Salt & Pepper & sear in a hot frying pan on both sides. Remove from the pan & set aside. Finely chop the Onions, Garlic Cloves & Carrots & add to the pan & cook until soft. Add the Flour & cook for another 2 minutes. Add the Wine & simmer until reduced by half. Add the Stock, Thyme & Bay Leaves. Transfer the Wine & Vegetables into a large ovenproof dish. Add the Duck, skin side down & cover with foil & cook for 50 minutes. Cut the Mushrooms into quarters & add to the dish & place a Rasher of Bacon on top of each leg. Return to the oven & cook for another 20 minutes.

Duck with Rosemary & Garlic

SERVES 4

Ingredients

4 Duck Breasts, 600g of New Potatoes, 8 Garlic Cloves, 8 Fresh Bay Leaves, Red Currant Sauce, 2tbsp. of Rosemary Leaves.

Method

Boil the kettle & heat the oven to 240°C. Add the Potatoes & peeled Garlic Cloves to a pan & cover with Boiled water. Salt well. Boil for 5 minutes, drain & place in a large roasting tin. Finely chop the Rosemary & sprinkle on the Potatoes with Salt & Pepper. Score the Duck Breasts & put in a roasting tin skin side up, screw up the Bay Leaves & rub over the Duck Skin, Place 2 Bay Leaves under each Duck Breast. Season & Roast for 5 minutes. Remove the Duck from the oven & pour the fat over the Potatoes, shake well so they are coated, pour off any excess & add the Duck to the tin, Cook for 20 minutes, turn the Duck after 10 minutes & baste. Once cooked drain any fat off & place the Potatoes on kitchen roll. Serve with Red Currant Jelly.

Duck with Honey, Soy & Ginger

SERVES 4

Ingredients

4 Duck Breasts, 250ml of Chicken Stock, 4tbsp. of Honey, 4 tbsp. of Soy Sauce, 4 tbsp. of Sake Wine, 2 tbsp. of Fresh Ginger, 1tbsp. of Lime Juice, 2tsp. of Tomato Puree, ½ tsp of Chilli Powder, ½ tsp. of Cayenne Powder, Salt & Pepper.

Method

Heat the Oven to 200°C. Score each Duck Breast through the skin. Rub the skin with Salt, Cayenne Powder & Pepper. Heat an ovenproof pan on the hob & lie the Duck Breasts skin side down & fry until brown. Remove the excess fat from the pan & turn the Duck Breasts over & cook for 2 minutes. Place the pan in the oven & cook until the meat has reached the desired cooking stage. Peel & grate the Ginger. Remove from the oven & cover with tin foil. Add the Stock, Soy Sauce, Sake, Ginger, Tomato Puree, Chilli Powder & Lime Juice to the frying pan & whisk on high heat, bring to the boil, reduce to a simmer until the sauce thickens. Slice the Duck Breasts & place on plate, pour over the sauce. I serve this with Egg Noodles & Mange Tout.

Pasta

Linguine Vongole

The first time I had this dish was in Ohio & I have been talking about it ever since. I found a recipe & played around with it until I got here.

Ingredients

OO, 1 packet of Linguine, 1 Garlic Clove, 2 tins of Clams, 1 small handful of Parsley, 1 small Red Chilli, Dried Chilli Flakes, ½ a glass of White Wine, 25g of Butter, 2 Litres of Chicken Stock, Parmesan, A touch of Double Cream, Salt & Pepper.

Method

Add a small glug of OO to a large frying pan or similar. Slice the Garlic as thinly as you can & add to the pan. Place on a low heat & cook slowly, DO NOT BURN. Finely chop the Red

Chilli & the Parsley & add to the pan. Stir in Parsley & the Dried Chilli Flakes. Drain & reserve the liquid from the Clam tins. Add the liquid to the pan. Place the lid on the pan or cover with foil for 5 minutes still on a low heat. Mince up one of the tins of Clams with a knife & add all the Clams & White Wine to the pan. Stir every now & then until the Wine evaporates. Remove from the heat. Add the Chicken Stock to a large pan & bring to the boil, add Salt & add the Linguine & follow the directions on the packet, stir for a minute to separate the strands. When the Pasta is cooked drain & reserve. Add the Pasta to the Clam mixture, put on a medium heat & stir until all the liquid has reduced. Add a large knob of Butter, a touch of Double Cream, stir well making sure all the ingredients are mixed, pour into a large bowl, & dress with more chopped Parsley.

Tagliatelli with Crab, Chilli & Coriander.

SERVES 4

This is an amazingly quick dish, a perfect lunch & it will make friends think that you have gone to a great deal of effort!

Ingredients

2 Litres of Chicken Stock, 1 packet of Spaghetti, 00, 1 Leek, 1 Red Chilli, 2 Garlic Cloves, 5cm piece Fresh Ginger, 4 Large Tomatoes, 400g of White Crab Meat, ½ glass of White Wine, Juice of ½ Lime, a Large Handful of Coriander & Salt & Pepper.

Method

Add the Chicken Stock to a large pan & bring to the boil. Add Salt, the Pasta & cook to the directions on the packet. Make a cross cut on the bottom of each Tomato. Boil the kettle

& pour the water into a bowl, adding the Tomatoes, leave for one minute, remove the skins, remove the seeds & cut into small cubes. Slice the Leek, finely chop the Chilli & thinly slice the Garlic & Ginger. Add a glug of OO to a large pan. Add the Leek, Chilli, Garlic & Ginger & cook for 5 minutes until softened. Add the Tomatoes, Crab & Wine. Cook slowly until the Wine reduces. Bring to a simmer, & cook for 10 mins until the Tomatoes are soft & the mixture becomes a sauce. When the Pasta is cooked, drain, reserving a little of the cooking stock. Add to the Crab & mix well. Squeeze ½ a Lime over the mix, stir well, chop the Coriander, lift the Pasta into bowl & scatter the Coriander over the top.

Makarounia Tou Forno

SERVES 6

This is amazingly special. I have tried to get this as close to the taste that I remember, & serve it with My Favourite Salad.

Ingredients

OO, 1 Large Onion, 1 Handful Parsley, 2 Garlic Cloves, 850g Minced Pork & Beef, 1 Packet of Halloumi, 2 Bay Leaves, 1 tsp. Ground Cinnamon, 400g tinned tomatoes, 1 Packet of Long Bucatini Pasta, 40g of Butter, 1/2 tsp. Dried Mint, 2 Litres of Chicken Stock, **White Sauce** 120g Butter, 125g Plain Flour, 1 Litre of Milk, 2 Eggs, ¼ tsp Ground Nutmeg, Salt & Pepper

Method

Add a glug of OO to a large non-stick pan, chop the Onion & cook until soft & golden. Add the Parsley & Garlic, stir well for 2 minutes & add the Meat. Cook until all the liquid has been absorbed & the Mince is turning brown. Season with Salt & Pepper, add the Bay Leaves & the

Cinnamon. Add Tomatoes & a cup of water, turn down the heat & cook for 10 minutes. Heat up the oven to 180°C. Pour the Chicken Stock into a large pan & bring to the boil. Add Salt & cook the Pasta to the directions on the Packet. Once cooked drain & pour into a large bowl. Grate the Halloumi. Stir in the butter & cover with the Dried Mint & half the grated Halloumi. Stir well. Place the Meat an ovenproof dish, covering the entire base, press down evenly so it compacts. Cover with the Pasta making sure all of the Meat is covered. Set aside while you make the White Sauce. Beat the eggs well, & add to the milk. Melt the butter in a pan. Stir in the flour & cook for a few minutes, stirring all the time, then add the Milk & Egg slowly, whisking while adding. When the sauce is smooth & not too stiff, add salt, pepper & the nutmeg. Bring to the boil, & reduce to a simmer for about 5 minutes, stirring all the time. You should have a very thick & smooth sauce. Pour this over the Pasta & Meat in the dish. Sprinkle the remaining Halloumi over the top and bake for 30-40 minutes until the top is golden. **Let it cool for an hour before serving so the White Sauce can set.**

Spaghetti with Piccolo Tomatoes & Basil
SERVES 4

One of my very favourite Pasta dishes. Sweet, simple, fast & easy, yet totally scrummy.

Ingredients

OO, 2 Garlic Cloves, 750g of Piccolo Tomatoes, 25 Basil Leaves, 1 tsp. of Caster Sugar, 350g of Spaghetti, A Large knob if Butter, Salt & Pepper.

Method

Boil the kettle. Add a large glug of OO to the base of a large frying pan. Peel the Garlic Cloves & add to the pan, heat slowly & cook until golden on both sides. Cut the Tomatoes in half & place 18 Basil Leaves on top of each other, roll up like a cigar & shred. Add the Tomatoes, Sugar, Basil to the pan, season well. Pour boiled water into a saucepan, salt well add the Spaghetti & cook to the instructions on the packet. Drain the Pasta, add the Butter, stir well. Add the Spaghetti to the frying pan with the Tomatoes –remove the Garlic Cloves–mix well & place in a Serving Dish. Shred the remaining Basil Leaves & scatter over the top. Eat with Garlic Ciabatta & Parmesan Cheese.

Fettucine with Mushroom Sauce
SERVES 4
Ingredients
OO, 1 Garlic Cloves, 50g of Porcini Mushrooms, 400g of Mixed Mushrooms, 1 Rosemary Stem, 1 glass of White Wine, 20g of Butter, Salt & Pepper.
Method
Boil the kettle. Soak the Porcini Mushrooms in almost boiled water for 25-30 minutes. Reserve the liquid & squeeze the Mushrooms. Chop the Mixed Mushrooms into small pieces. Add a large glug of OO to the base of a frying pan. Finely chop the Garlic Clove, strip the Rosemary Stem, add to the pan & cook for 30 seconds. Add the Mushrooms to the pan along with the Porcini liquor, Wine, Butter & cook for gently for 20 minutes. Cook the Fettucine in boiled salted to the instructions on the packet. Drain the Pasta once cooked & add the Mushrooms, mixing well.

Sides

+Fasolia

Ingredients

500g Tinned Large White Beans, 1 Large Onion, 3 Carrots, 3 Celery Sticks, ½ tin of Chopped Tomatoes, 2 tbsp. Tomato Puree, 5 tbsp. OO, 2 Bay Leaves, Handful of Fresh Flat-Leaf Parsley, Salt & Pepper.

Method

Rinse & drain the Beans. Add to a pan of boiled water & cook for 5 minutes. Roughly chop the Onion, peel & slice the Carrot & add to the pan. Stir for 2 minutes, & add the Tomatoes & the Bay Leaves. Simmer for half an hour. Allow to cool slightly, season with Salt & Pepper. This can be served as a side or on its own.

Mushroom & Potato Bake

Ingredients

OO, 1kg of New Potatoes, 1 Large Onion, 500g of Mixed Mushrooms, 25g of Porcini Mushrooms, 4 Garlic Cloves, 3 tbsp. of Tomato Puree, Fresh Thyme, Fresh Parsley, 600ml of White Wine, 600ml of Vegetable Stock, 600ml of Double Cream, 1 pack of Baby Spinach, 200g of Gruyere Cheese, 150g of Parmesan, Salt & Pepper.

Method

Boil the kettle. Heat the oven to 200°C. Scrub the Potatoes & dry well. Add a large glug of OO to a roasting tin, add the Potatoes & toss until coating in OO. Cook in the oven for 40 minutes until golden. Cover the Porcini Mushrooms with boiled water & sit for 15 minutes. Remove from the liquid & set aside. Chop the Onion & mixed Mushrooms roughly along with the Porcini. Add a glug of OO to a large pan, add the Onion & Mushrooms. Crush the Garlic & add to the pan. Add the Tomato Puree, 1tbsp. of Fresh Thyme Leaves & the White Wine. Bring to the boil & simmer for 2 minutes. Add the Stock, Cream & simmer for 20 minutes until reduced. Drain the Potatoes. Add to an oven proof dish, pour over the Mushrooms & Cream mixture. Add the Gruyere Cheese & grate the Parmesan adding half. Place in the Oven, cook for 20 minutes. Remove from oven & sprinkle with the remaining Parmesan, chopped Parsley & Thyme Leaves.

New Potato & Garlic Crush

Ingredients
500g of New Potatoes, 6 Garlic Cloves, 30g of Butter, Salt & Pepper.

Method
Fill the Kettle & put it on to boil. Wash the Potatoes & place in a large Pan covering with the Boiled Water. Peel the Garlic Cloves & add to the pan. Salt well. Bring the water to the boil, reduce to a simmer & cook until the Potatoes are soft but not breaking. Drain & leave in the Colander for 5 minutes covered with a tea towel. Remove the Garlic Cloves, add to a bowl, & squash with a fork until they becoming a paste. Add the Butter & mix well. Transfer the Potatoes into a serving dish & squash with a fork, adding some of the Garlic Butter. Serve immediately.

Halloumi with Tomatoes & Oregano

This is wonderful. You have to make lots as once people have tried it, they want more.

Ingredients

OO, 3 Packets of Halloumi, 3 Beef Tomatoes, Fresh Oregano Leaves & Black Pepper.

Method

Lightly drizzle the bottom of a Roasting Tin with OO. Slice the Halloumi into 1cm thick pieces & place in a roasting tray. Slice the Beef Tomatoes & place on top of the Halloumi. Sprinkle with Oregano Leaves & season with Black Pepper. Place under the grill until the Halloumi starts to brown. Serve immediately & eat whilst hot.

Mash Potato with Garlic & Basil

SERVES 4

Ingredients

500g of Maris Piper Potatoes, 6 Garlic Cloves, 10 Fresh Basil Leaves, 30g of Butter, a splash of Milk, Salt & Pepper.

Method

Boil the Kettle. Peel the Potatoes & cut into golf ball size pieces. Peel the Garlic, lie on a chopping board & hit with the flat of a large knife & your hand. Pour the boiled water into a pan, put on a high heat & return to the boil. Salt well. Add Potatoes & Garlic & bring the boil, reduce the heat & simmer until the Potatoes are softened but not falling apart. Drain & leave in the colander. I use a ricer or pass the Potatoes through a sieve to mash my veg, so either use these for the Potatoes & Garlic or use a traditional masher. Add the Butter, a splash of Milk & season with Salt & Pepper. Chop the Basil Leaves & stir into the Potatoes & Garlic.

Stilton & Mushrooms on Toast

SERVES 6

Ingredients

OO, 6 slices of Bloomer Loaf, 500g of Button Mushrooms, 75g of Butter, 2 Garlic Cloves, 75g of Stilton Cheese, 200ml of Chicken Stock, 75ml of Double Cream, Salt & Black Pepper.

Method

Gently melt the Butter in a pan. Wipe any dirt from the Mushrooms, add to the pan & cook for 5 minutes. Remove from the pan & place on kitchen roll. Heat up the grill. Place the Bread under the grill & cook both sides until golden. Rub one side of the bread with a Garlic Clove. Heat the Chicken Stock in a saucepan until boiling. Add the Cream, crumble in the Stilton & cook, stirring constantly, over a low heat for 1-2 minutes, or until the sauce has thickened. Add the Mushrooms & cook for a further 2 minutes. Spoon the Mushroom & Sauce onto the bread & place back under the grill for 1 minute. Serve immediately.

The Most Amazing Italian Red Sauce

This takes time but you will understand why once you have tasted it! I make it in huge batches so I can freeze it & use it whenever I wish.

Ingredients

40 On The Vine Large Tomatoes (I buy these from Aldi as they are extremely good value) 2 Large Red Onions, Fresh Basil, 100ml of Water, 2 Large Garlic Cloves, 3 tbsp. Tomato Purée, Pinch of Sugar, Salt & Pepper.

Method

Cut the Tomatoes in half, roughly chop the Red Onions & add to a large deep pan. Add 100ml of Cold Water & add three stems of Basil Leaves. Cover the pan with the lid & simmer on a low heat until the Tomatoes have cooked down, for 1 hour. Allow to cool overnight. Pass the Tomatoes, Onions & Basil through a sieve into a clean pan. Season with Salt & Pepper & bring to a slow boil & reduce to a simmer. Add the Tomato Purée & Garlic Cloves. Simmer until the Garlic Cloves are soft & cooked all the way through. Check the seasoning & add a large pinch of sugar to take away the sharpness of the tomatoes. Use a hand blender to blitz. Adjust the seasoning. Allow to cool before transferring freezer bags.

Asparagus with Prosciutto & Cheese Sauce

Ingredients

24 Asparagus Spears, 24 Pieces of Prosciutto, 75g of Butter, 150g of Plain Flour, 1 Litre of room temperature Full Cream Milk, Salt ,Pepper, 100g of Cheddar, Grated Mozzarella & Parmesan Cheese.

Method

Remove the hard part of the stalks from the Asparagus stems. Wash & pat dry. Wrap each Asparagus Spear with a piece of Prosciutto & place in an ovenproof dish in two layers. Heat the oven to 180°C. Make the White Sauce – Melt the butter in a saucepan, add the flour & allow to cook for a few minutes, stirring constantly. Slowly add the Milk, & stir until the sauce begins to thicken, (you can stop adding the milk). Remove from the heat & grate the Cheese, & add ¾ to the pan, stir well whilst the Cheese is melting. Pour over the Asparagus, & scatter the remaining Cheese over the top. Place in the oven for 20minutes until the top is golden & bubbling.

Tashi (Dashi) Dip

This is by far my favourite dip of any I have ever tried. This is a memory from a childhood trip to Cyprus & stayed with me until I tasted it again 20 years later.

Ingredients

3tbsp. of Tahini Paste, 3 tbsp. of Water, 1 Garlic Clove, Juice of Half a Lemon & Salt.

Method

In a bowl add the Tahini Paste & a little of the Water. Stir slowly until it begins to thicken. Add a squeeze of lemon Juice. Smash the Garlic & keep chopping until extremely fine. Stir into the mix. Add Salt to taste.

Rosemary Potatoes

SERVES 4

Ingredients

OO, 500g of White Potatoes, Rosemary, Salt & Pepper.

Method

Boil the kettle, peel the potatoes & cut into small cubes about 2cm square. Heat the oven up to 180°C. Add to a pan, cover with boiled water, Salt well, bring to the boil & simmer until just tender. Drain well & shake in a colander. Add a glug of OO to a roasting tin & shred the Rosemary Stems over the top. Mix well, add the Potatoes, drizzle with OO, mix, season with Salt & Pepper. Cook for 25 minutes until golden.

Roasted Aubergine & Pepper Dip

Ingredients

OO, 1 Aubergine, 2 Red Peppers, 1 Red Onion, 2 Garlic Cloves, Salt & Pepper

Method

Heat oven to 180°C. Roughly chop the Aubergine, Peppers & Onion. Peel the Garlic Cloves. Place all the Vegetables on a Roasting Tin, drizzle with OO & season. Roast for 45 minutes, until just coloured. Allow to cool for 10 minutes. Add all of the Vegetables to a Blender, loosen with OO & pulse until smooth. Season with Salt & Pepper. Dip away!

Fakes – Lentils with Vinegar

Ingredients

OO, 250g of Brown Lentils, 1 Onion, 2 Garlic Cloves, 1tbsp. of Tomato Puree, 2 tbsp. Vinegar, 2 Bay Leaves, 1 Litre of Water, Salt & Pepper.

Method

Boil the Kettle. Add the Lentils to the pan & cover with boiled water & cook for 5 minutes & repeat. Slice the Onion into rings, add to the pan along with the peeled but whole Garlic Cloves, the Bay Leaves & Tomato Puree. Simmer for 10 minutes. Add 100ml of OO, Salt & Pepper, return to the boil & simmer for 30 minutes. Drain & add to a serving dish. Add Vinegar to taste & mix well. This can be eaten hot or cold.

Olive Dip

Ingredients

OO, 400g of Black Pitted Olives, 2 Garlic Cloves, Salt & Pepper.

Method

Heat the oven to 200°C. Place the Garlic Cloves (unpeeled) in the oven & cook for 15 minutes. Remove from the oven & allow to cool. Place the Olives into a Blender, squeeze the Garlic from the skins & add to the Olives. Loosen with OO & pulse until smooth. Season with Salt & Pepper. Dip!

Tomato shots with Herby Yoghurt Cream

SERVES 4

Ingredients

OO, 500g of Ripe soft Tomatoes, 1 Onion, 200ml of Vegetable Stock, 2 Garlic Cloves, 2 tsp. Chipotle Sauce, Thick Greek Yoghurt, 15 Basil Leaves, 2 Rosemary Stems, Salt & Pepper.

Method

Heat the oven to 160°C. Chop the Onion & slice the Tomatoes in half. Add to a roasting tin with the unpeeled Garlic. Coat with OO, add the Rosemary Stems & season. Roast for 1 hour until soft. Remove from the oven, remove the Rosemary, place the Vegetables in a blender & pulse until smooth. Sieve the liquid. Add the Vegetable Stock to the liquid with the Chipotle Sauce. Check the seasoning, adjust & place in the fridge for 2 hours. Mix well. . Place 10 Basil Leaves on top of each other, rollup like a cigar & finely shred. Add to a bowl & top with 150ml of Thick Greek Yoghurt Pour the Tomato mix into shot glasses, spoon a thick layer of the Yoghurt on top, shred the remaining Basil Leaves & scatter over the top. Serve.

Roasted Red Peppers with Halloumi

Ingredients

OO, 6 Red Peppers, 4 Garlic Cloves, 250g of Halloumi, 15 Mint Leaves, the Juice & Zest of a Lemon, 1 tbsp. of Fresh Thyme Leaves, 4 tbsp. of Pine Nuts, Salt & Pepper.

Method

Heat the oven to 200°C. Cut the Peppers in half from top to bottom, removing all the seeds & any pith. Drizzle the skin side of the Peppers & the bottom of a Roasting tin. Add the Peppers, flesh side up & set aside. Thinly slice the Garlic,

Halloumi, Zest & grate the Lemon, place the Mint Leaves on top of each other, roll up like a cigar & finely shred. Place half of the Garlic in the Peppers, adding the Halloumi, Mint Leaves, Lemon Zest, the remainder of the Garlic, Thyme Leaves & Pine Nuts. Season with Salt & Pepper, drizzle with OO & the Lemon Juice. Cook for 30 minutes until golden.

Wonderful Bread, Cheese & Meat

This is a fantastic beginning to an Italian style feast.

Ingredients

OO, 100g Prosciutto, 6 slices of Fresh Bread, 2 Garlic Cloves, 100g Mozzarella, 225g of Cherry or Piccolo Tomatoes, Parsley, Salt & Pepper.

Method

Chop the Mozzarella, Prosciutto, quarter the Tomatoes & place in a bowl, chop the Parsley & add 3tbsp. to the bowl & mix together. Toast the Bread on both sides, remove from the heat & rub both sides with a Garlic Clove, drizzle the top with OO & cover with the Mozzarella mix. Place back under the grill until the cheese has melted.

Cakes

Triple Chocolate Brownies

Once you have made these & given them to friends & family you may find yourself with marriage proposals & promises to love you forever – Don't be misled they only want you for your Brownies.

Ingredients

250g of Unsalted Butter, 350g of Dark 70% Cocoa Solids Chocolate, 115g of Plain Flour, 50g of Cocoa Powder, 4 Eggs, 375g of Soft Brown Sugar, 100g of Milk Chocolate, 100g White Chocolate,75g of Fudge & Full Cream Milk.

Method

Heat the oven to 160°. Break the Eggs & add to a large bowl

with the Soft Brown Sugar & using an electric whisk beat until thick & creamy. Melt the Butter & 250g Dark Chocolate together. Chop all the Chocolate & Fudge into small pieces, (you can reduce all of the Quantities to 75g & add 75g of Walnuts if you would like to) keep cool. Once the Eggs & Sugar mix is thick & creamy, add the melted Chocolate & Butter to the mix & fold in. Once mixed add the Flour & the Cocoa Powder to the mix via a sieve. Fold in until all the Flour is mixed. Add the chopped Chocolate & Fudge & mix in well. If very thick add a little Full Cream Milk. Grease the inside of a square, deep roasting tin & line with Greaseproof Paper. Pour the mix into the tin & place in the oven for 55 minutes. Remove from oven & allow to cool for at least two hours. Remove from the tin & place on a wire rack. Cut into slices & serve. These are also totally stupendous with Custard or Cream.

My Mum's Whisked Sponge

My Mum used to make this for her charity BBQ's & it was always greatly appreciated.

Ingredients

3 Eggs, 75g of Caster Sugar, 75g of Plain Flour, 20 Strawberries, Strawberry Jam & 500ml of Double Cream.

Method

Grease & line the cake tin or tins. Whisk the Eggs & Sugar together until thick & creamy. Heat the oven to 190°C. Cook for 10 minutes until the sponge feels springy to the touch & allow to cool. Once cool remove from the tin(s). If only using one tin slice the sponge through the middle, & place the top layer aside. Cover the bottom sponge with a thick even layer of Strawberry Jam. Whisk the Double Cream until thick & forming peaks. Spread 2/3 of the Cream over the top of the

Jam. Place the top sponge on the Cream & cover with the remaining Cream. Decorate the top with Strawberries cut into halves.

Praline Swiss Roll

Ingredients

3 Eggs, 125g Soft Brown Sugar, 75g of Plain Flour, 1tbsp. Hot Water. 125g Unsalted Butter, 250g Icing Sugar, 25g of Un-Blanched Almonds, 2tbsp. Milk & ½ tsp. Vanilla Extract.

Method

Heat the oven to 200°C. Grease & line a flat baking tray. Whisk the Eggs & Sugar together until thick & creamy. Sieve the Flour & Coffee Powder into the mix & fold in well. Add the Water & fold in. Pour onto the tray & cook for 10 minutes until the sponge feels springy & allow to cool. Once cooled roll up. Grease a baking tray. Place the Sugar & Almonds in a pan until the Sugar melts & the Almonds begin to split. Pour onto the baking tray. Allow to cool & break up into small pieces. Add half of the Icing Sugar & mix in well. Add the remaining Icing Sugar & Milk & mix until the mixture is thick & creamy. Add a touch more Milk to loosen if too thick. Unroll the Sponge & mix the Sugar & Almonds into the Butter Icing. Spread the Icing in a layer over the sponge & reroll. Cut into slices & serve.

My Mum's Coffee & Walnut Cake

This is the first cake I made following Mum's directions. I was very pleased with how it turned out. I like to add chopped Walnuts to the cake mix & decorate with Coffee Butter Cream & Walnuts.

Ingredients

2 Eggs, 100g Stork, 100g of Caster Sugar, 150g Self Raising Flour, 2tsp. Baking Powder, 2 tbsp. of Camp Coffee, Milk, 200g of Walnut Halves, 125g Unsalted Butter, 250g Icing Sugar, 1-2 tbsp. Milk, ½ tsp of Camp Coffee.

Method

Heat the oven to 150°C. Cream the Stock & Sugar together until light & creamy. Add the Eggs & mix well. Sieve the Flour & Baking Powder into the mix & blend well until all the ingredients are combined. Add the Camp Coffee, mix well & add Milk to thin out the mixture. Grease & line the cake or loaf tin. Pour in the mixture & cook for 45 minutes. Remove from the oven & allow to cool. Beat the butter in a large bowl until soft. Add half of the Icing Sugar & mix in until smooth. Add the remaining Icing Sugar & Milk & mix until the mixture is thick & creamy. Add a touch more Milk to loosen if too thick. Add the Camp Coffee. Once the Cake is cooled spread the Butter Icing over the top & decorate with Walnut Halves.

Eton Mess

SERVES 4

The simplest scrummy dessert, with lots of berries.

Ingredients

4 Meringue Nests, Mascarpone Cheese, Double Cream, Caster Sugar to sweeten & Fresh Berries.

Method

Whip the Cream & Mascarpone Cheese together until smooth. Crunch up the Meringue Nest & add to the Cream mix. Fold in until all mixed well. Add half the Berries & Mix well. Transfer into bowls & dress with the remaining Berries. Yummy Yum Yum.

Index

Salads

Soups

Mains

Chicken

Beef

Pork

Sides & Stuff

Cakes

Photo by Errol McQuinn

7259495R00045

Printed in Great Britain
by Amazon.co.uk, Ltd.,
Marston Gate.